Let's Look at the Seasons

Wintertime

By Ann Schweninger

PUFFIN BOOKS

721811

PUFFIN BOOKS
Published by the Penguin Group
Penguin Books USA Inc., 375 Hudson Street, New York, New York 10014, U.S.A.
Penguin Books Ltd, 27 Wrights Lane, London W8 5TZ, England
Penguin Books Australia Ltd, Ringwood, Victoria, Australia
Penguin Books Canada Ltd, 10 Alcorn Avenue, Toronto, Ontario, Canada M4V 3B2
Penguin Books (N.Z.) Ltd, 182–190 Wairau Road, Auckland 10, New Zealand

Penguin Books Ltd, Registered Offices: Harmondsworth, Middlesex, England

First published in the United States of America by Viking Penguin,
a division of Penguin Books USA Inc., 1990
Published in Puffin Books, 1993

1   3   5   7   9   10   8   6   4   2

LIBRARY OF CONGRESS CATALOGING-IN-PUBLICATION DATA
Schweninger, Ann.
Wintertime / by Ann Schweninger.
p.   cm. — (Let's look at the seasons)
Summary: A dog family explores the changes
that happen in nature during the winter.
ISBN 0-14-054286-8
1. Winter—Juvenile literature. [1. Winter. 2. Nature.]
I. Title. II. Series: Schweninger, Ann. Let's look at the seasons.
[QB637.8.S38 1993]
574.5'43—dc20   93-16685   CIP   AC

Printed in the United States of America
Set in Cheltenham Book

For Barbara Hennessy and Deborah Brodie

First Day

DECEMBER 21

Let's go outside!

The first day of winter is December 21st. The sun rises later, and sets earlier, than on any other day of the year.

Early Winter

Winter is the coldest time of year. The earth is farthest away from the warmth of the sun.

Rabbits live in old burrows dug by woodchucks or skunks. They eat twigs and buds.

Chipmunks dig their own little tunnels to live in and store seeds for food.

Squirrels live in nests in hollow trees. They bury nuts in the ground, to dig up when they are hungry.

A woodchuck closes the opening to its burrow to keep out the cold air. The woodchuck, sometimes called a groundhog, sleeps all winter.

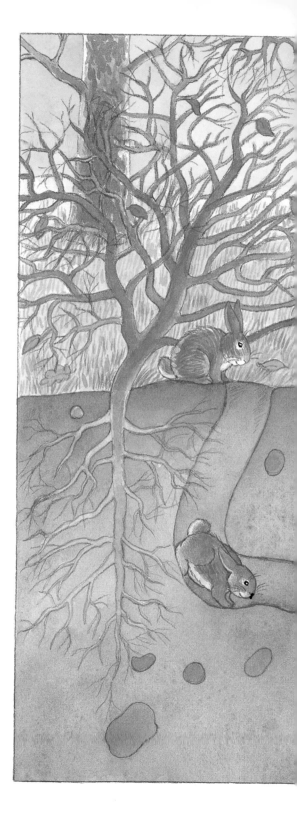

Frost and Ice

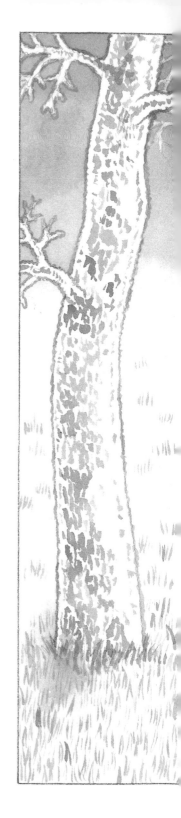

When the temperature falls below 32°, dew and moisture become frost. Water freezes and turns to ice.

Sometimes ice melts, drips, and freezes again. Then icicles are made.

Have you heard of Jack Frost? Stories tell us that he crosses the land, covering it with frost.

Animals in Winter

During winter some animals go to warmer places where there is plenty of food.

California gray whales migrate. So do monarch butterflies.

Other animals sleep all winter, usually underground or inside a cave.

Grizzly bears hibernate all winter. So do bats, turtles, and snails.

Some animals stay on through the cold winter.

Animals with fur grow thick long coats to stay warm.
Deer grow warm coats. So do raccoons and foxes.
Birds fluff their feathers to stay warm.

Making a Bird Feeder

Here's what you need: a pinecone

peanut butter   a butter knife

bird seed   wax paper

scissors   string

Cut a piece of string about 8 inches long.

Tie the string to the large end of the pinecone.

Use the butter knife to put small amounts* of peanut butter on the petals of the pinecone.

*Birds cannot swallow too much peanut butter at one time.

Spread a piece of wax paper and pour some birdseed onto it.

Roll the pine-cone in the seed.

Hang it up where wild birds will find it.

Once you begin to feed wild birds, they count on you, so please keep feeding them all through the winter.

Winter Tree

During winter, a tree rests. Its leaves have fallen and sap has left the branches.

The branches have winter buds. The buds are made of tiny folded leaves.

Even the roots are resting. They do not grow during the winter.

Tough scales protect the outside of the buds.

Happy New Year!

Take the old
calendar down . . .

. . . and hang up a
new one!

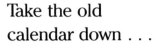

At midnight on December 31st,
the old year ends,
and the New Year begins.

January

warm coats

wooly hats

cozy mittens

winter boots

long scarves

Snuggly snowsuit

bulky sweater

heavy sweatshirt

thick socks

It's snowing outside!

Bundle, pull, struggle. Snuggle, wrap. Snap, snap, snap!

Snow

A snowflake begins . . .

                   . . . as a drop of water . . .

      . . . that falls from a cloud.

In the cold air . . .

                 . . . the water freezes . . .

             . . . and becomes a snowflake.

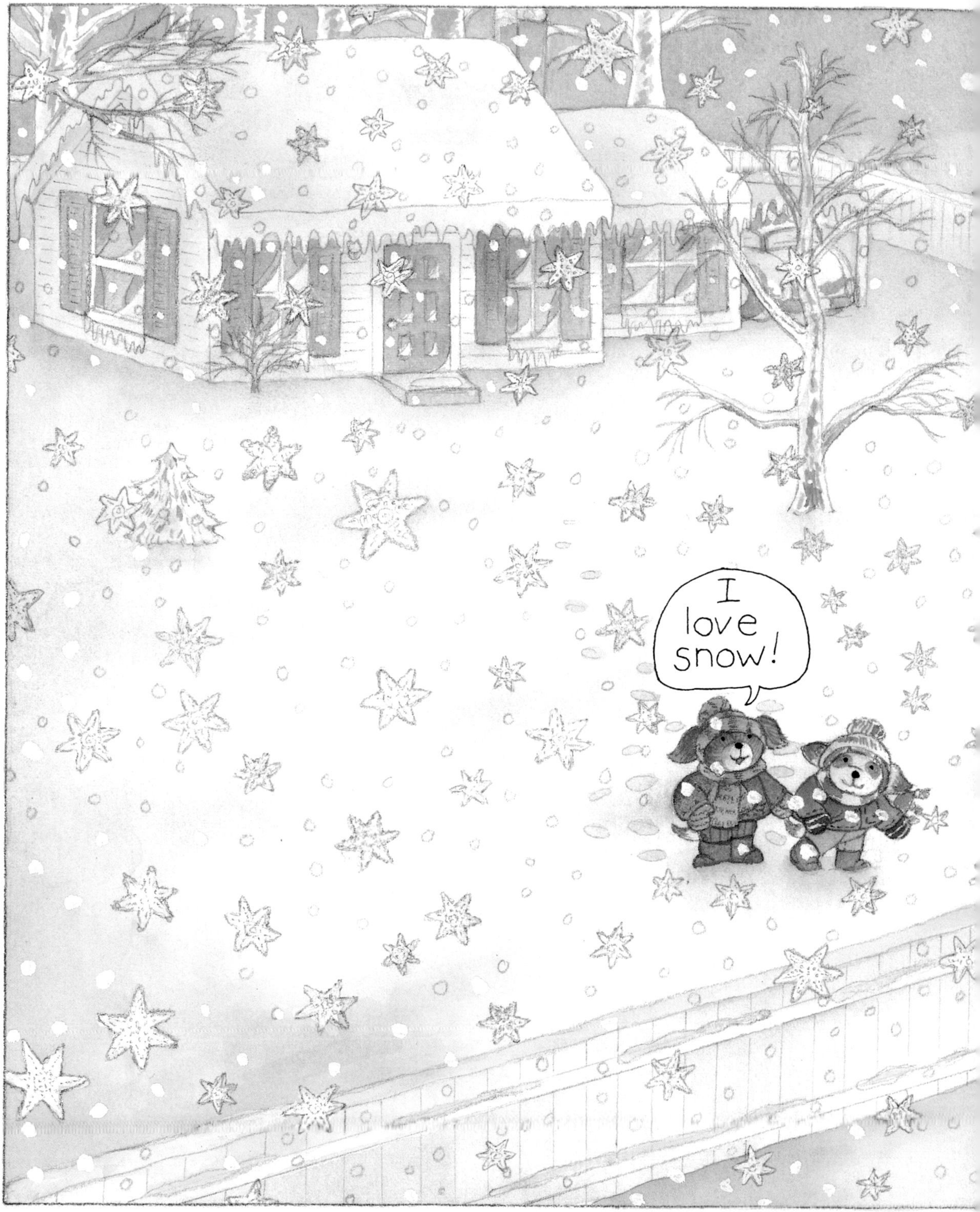
I love snow!

A Different Winter

In a warm climate, there is no snow. During winter, it sometimes rains and is breezy.

Flowers bloom outdoors and orange trees grow fruit all winter long.

The farther north you live, the longer winter is. The farther south you live, the shorter winter is.

Groundhog Day

Legend says, if the groundhog comes out of his burrow and sees his shadow, there will be six more weeks of winter. If he does not see his shadow, there will be an early spring.

Shadow!

No shadow!

A Nature Hunt

When you see animal tracks, think about what animal
has paws or feet that are like the tracks.

Where are the tracks? Tracks near a hedge may be made
by a wild rabbit.

Look for other clues. A hole in the ground and broken
nutshells may mean that a squirrel has dug up a nut.

Raccoon

Mouse

Bird

Deer

Skunk

Cottontail Rabbit

Fox

Squirrel

Valentine's Day

March

As winter ends, the earth moves closer to the sun. Days are warmer and longer.

Sap runs in trees again and leaf buds are plump, waiting to open.

Birds that flew south begin to return.

Underground, it seems that all is quiet, but daffodil and tulip bulbs are beginning to grow.